Art Profiles For Kids

VINCENT VAN GOGH

Mitchell Lane
PUBLISHERS

P.O. Box 196
Hockessin, Delaware 19707
Visit us on the web: www.mitchelllane.com
Comments? email us: mitchelllane@mitchelllane.com

ART PROFILES FOR KIDS

Titles in the Series

Art Profiles For Kids

VINCENT VAN GOGH

Jim Whiting

P.O. Box 196
Hockessin, Delaware 19707
Visit us on the web: www.mitchelllane.com
Comments? email us: mitchelllane@mitchelllane.com

Printing   1   2   3   4   5   6   7   8   9

Library of Congress Cataloging-in-Publication Data

Whiting, Jim, 1943–
  Vincent Van Gogh / by Jim Whiting.
     p. cm.— (Art profiles for kids)
  Includes bibliographical references and index.
  ISBN 978-1-58415-564-5 (library bound)
  1. Gogh, Vincent van, 1853–1890—Juvenile literature. 2. Painters—Netherlands—Biography—Juvenile literature. I. Gogh, Vincent van, 1853-1890. II. Title.
  ND653.G7W46 2007
  759.9492—dc22
                                                                    2007000662

ABOUT THE AUTHOR: Jim Whiting has been a remarkably versatile and accomplished journalist, writer, editor, and photographer for more than 30 years. He has long been fascinated by the works of Vincent van Gogh and has seen many firsthand. A voracious reader since early childhood, Mr. Whiting has written and edited over 200 nonfiction children's books, including *William Shakespeare, Hercules,* and *Michelangelo* for Mitchell Lane Publishers. He lives in Washington State with his wife and two teenage sons.

ABOUT THE COVER: The images on the cover are paintings by the various artists in this series.

PHOTO CREDITS: Except for images in sidebar stories, all images are the work of Vincent van Gogh.

PUBLISHER'S NOTE: The facts on which this story is based have been thoroughly researched. Documentation of such research appears on page 45. While every possible effort has been made to ensure accuracy, the publisher will not assume liability for damages caused by inaccuracies in the data, and makes no warranty on the accuracy of the information contained herein.

PLB

Table of Contents

Art Profiles for Kids

Vincent Van Gogh's painting *Portrait of Dr. Gachet* caused a sensation in the art world when it sold at auction in May 1990 for more than $80 million. Van Gogh painted it in June 1890, almost exactly a century before its sale. Dr. Gachet's hand rests next to a foxglove. Digitalis is extracted from this plant and used to treat heart conditions, so using it in the painting identifies Gachet as a physician.

one

A Record-Breaking Painting

Many people believe that records are made to be broken. Whether it's Hank Aaron's lifetime 755 home runs or something from the *Guinness Book of World Records* (such as 4,079,381 dominoes toppled in a row), people are always eager to witness new all-time bests.

That was the main reason a crowd of well-dressed art lovers began arriving in the early evening of May 15, 1990, at Christie's auction house in New York City. About two and a half years earlier, a painting called *Irises* had been auctioned off for $53.9 million. That reflected the actual sale price of $49 million plus a 10 percent commission. It was the highest price that had ever been paid for a work of art at an auction. The previous record had been established earlier in 1987 when *Sunflowers* attracted a bid of just under $40 million.

Now there was an excited buzz of anticipation. About sixty works of art were being auctioned off this evening. Most of the interest centered on a portrait that had been painted almost exactly one hundred years previously. It was entitled *Portrait of Dr. Gachet.* It wasn't a very large painting, measuring 26 inches high by 22 inches wide. The artist was Vincent van Gogh, who had also painted *Irises* and *Sunflowers.*

Soon the main auction room was packed. Every one of the 600 chairs was occupied. At least 100 more people stood along the sides and at the back. Reporters from major newspapers and art magazines also managed to squeeze in. TV camera crews set up their equipment.

I think, or shall we say just as much, so that's that. Now when one blind man leads another blind man, don't they both fall into the ditch."[4]

Professionally it was a very different story. Van Gogh began the painting on June 3, 1890. It took him only two or three days to finish. The painting embodied everything that Van Gogh had learned about painting portraits.

He deliberately posed Dr. Gachet leaning on one arm, his upper body stretched diagonally across the canvas, to represent sadness. For Van Gogh, sadness was "the heartbroken expression of our time."[5]

In a way, it wasn't a portrait of the doctor at all. The painting doesn't really resemble existing photographs of Gachet. Rather, Van Gogh was using his model to represent the way that many people felt during the end of the nineteenth century. They were outwardly prosperous and inwardly sad.

"Nervous, fast-paced strokes, moving in parallel patterns, fill the canvas with electric anxiety that seems to travel directly from the doctor's brain," says Saltzman. "Van Gogh transcribed a sense of despair in the deep stained-glass tint of the jacket and the other tones of blue."[6]

To the subject, at least, the painting was a success. "Gachet liked it so much that he asked Van Gogh to paint a second version of the portrait," notes art historian Ingo Walther. "Art was a strong bond in their friendship and Van Gogh was overjoyed, at long last, to paint someone who really understood his work."[7]

"I've done the portrait of M. Gachet with a melancholy expression," he wrote to his sister a week after he had completed the painting, "which might well seem like a grimace to those who see it. And yet I had to paint it like that to convey how much expression and passion there is in our present-day heads in comparison with the old calm portraits, and how much longing and crying out."[8]

Van Gogh was no stranger to "longing and crying out." It was his tragedy to lead a life that consisted largely of mental and emotional suffering. It was his genius to be able to channel this suffering into some of the greatest art the world has ever known.

An Expensive Vanishing Act

When the gavel on the sale of *Portrait of Dr. Gachet* went down, the curtain went up on a great mystery. The painting quickly crossed the Pacific Ocean to Japan, where its new owner—Ryoei Saito—reportedly spent several hours looking at it. Then he locked it in a secret vault.

Within a few years, Saito's vast industrial empire—the source of his immense wealth—crumbled. In 1993, he was charged with bribing local officials into allowing him to establish a golf course, which he planned to call Vincent. He received a suspended sentence.

Saito's physical condition was also crumbling. Near death, he said he wanted to burn the painting and bury its ashes with him. People all over the world were shocked and horrified. Later Saito said that he was just joking.

When he died in 1996, the mystery deepened. It wasn't clear who owned the painting—the people to whom Saito owed money or his heirs. In addition, only a handful of people knew where it was, and they weren't talking.

There is strong evidence that the painting was eventually sold to an Austrian named Wolfgang Flöttl, who, like Saito, found himself in legal hot water and had to sell the painting. At this point, the trail grows cold. No one knows who owns the painting or where it is.

Even before Saito bought the painting, *Portrait of Dr. Gachet* had a history of vanishing. It was sold several times before a German art museum bought it in 1911. When Nazi dictator Adolf Hitler assumed power in 1933,

the museum director hid it because the Nazis didn't approve of the style in which it was painted. Four years later, authorities found it and gave it to Hitler's associate Hermann Goering, who sold it to buy more "acceptable" art. The purchaser was Siegfried Kramarsky, and the painting remained in his family until its 1990 sale.

The Kramarskys often loaned it to museums. Many people hope that whoever now owns the painting will be as generous so that art lovers can again view this Van Gogh masterpiece.

U.S. generals in 1945 recover art that had been stolen by the Nazis.

Van Gogh painted many self-portraits. This one, painted in 1889 and entitled *Self-Portrait with Palette,* is one of a comparative handful in which Van Gogh depicted himself with the tools of his artistic trade.

Early Struggles

Theodorus and Anna Carbentus van Gogh were relieved when their son, Vincent Willem van Gogh, was born healthy on March 30, 1853. Exactly one year before, their first child, whom they had also named Vincent, had been stillborn. The second Vincent became the first of six children. Anna (born in 1855), Theodorus ("Theo," 1857), Elisabeth (1859), Willemina (1862), and Cornelis (1866) rounded out the family.

The Van Goghs lived in the Dutch village of Groot-Zundert, in the province of North Brabant. Theodorus was the pastor of the local church, while his wife took care of the household.

Hardly anything is known about Vincent's early years, except that he apparently had a happy childhood. "Little Vincent had a great love for animals and flowers, and made all kinds of collections," his sister-in-law Johanna van Gogh-Bonger remembered. "There was as yet no sign of any extraordinary gift for drawing; it was only noted that at the age of eight he once modelled a little clay elephant that drew his parents' attention, but he destroyed it at once when, according to his notion, such a fuss was made about it. The same fate befell a very curious drawing of a cat, which his mother always remembered."[1]

It's likely that he enjoyed playing outside, in a natural environment. "[Vincent and Theo's] childhood was full of the poetry of Brabant country life; they grew up among the wheatfields, the heath and the pine forests, in that peculiar sphere of a village parsonage, the charm of which remained with them all their lives," Van Gogh-Bonger added. "It was not perhaps the best training to fit them for the hard struggle that awaited them both; they were still so very young when they had to go out into the world, and during the years following, with what bitter melancholy and inexpressible homesickness did they long for the sweet home in the little village on the heath."[2]

Vincent probably began attending the local school when he was about seven or eight. When he was eleven, his parents decided to send him to boarding school. It was located in the town of Zevenbergen, about twenty miles from Groot-Zundert. Two years later he began attending a secondary school in the town of Tilburg. He stayed there for a year and a half, but didn't graduate. Perhaps his parents couldn't afford to keep him there.

Soon it was time for him to get a job. He didn't have to look very hard. Three of his father's brothers were all involved in the art business. His uncle Vincent, also known as Cent, was the most successful. He was a partner in an important firm of art dealers called Goupil and Company. In 1869, when Vincent was sixteen, Uncle Cent arranged for him to start working for Goupil in its office in The Hague, one of the largest cities in The Netherlands. Establishing the boy in the art trade seemed to be a natural choice. Uncle Cent was especially close to Vincent's father—they had been born only a year apart. The bond was even closer because they had married two sisters.

In August 1872, Vincent's brother Theo—then fifteen—visited him for several days in The Hague. The two began writing regularly to each other. It was a practice they would maintain for the rest of their lives. These letters have become especially valuable, because they provide the major source of information about what Vincent was doing, feeling, and thinking at important times of his life.

In 1873, Vincent transferred to Goupil's London office. It was probably a promotion. He seemed destined to become successful as an art dealer.

At first he was happy there. He read a great deal and studied art history. This also seems to be the time that he began to draw. "I am quite contented," he wrote Theo soon after his arrival. "I walk much, the neighborhood where I live is quiet, pleasant, and fresh, and I was really very lucky in finding it. . . . I am doing very well, and it is a great pleasure for me to study London and the English way of living and the English people themselves; and then I have nature and art and poetry, and if that is not enough, what is enough?"[3]

Later he wrote, "Try to walk as much as you can, and keep your love for nature, for that is the true way to learn to understand art more and more. Painters understand nature and love her and teach us to see her. If one really loves nature, one can find beauty everywhere."[4]

His rosy view of life soon changed, though he didn't tell Theo about it. He fell in love with Eugenie Loyer, his landlady's daughter. Unfortunately for Vincent, she was secretly engaged to another man. She refused to have anything to do with him in spite of all his pleading. She broke his heart. Some scholars believe that this failed relationship began the depression that would later plague him.

In 1875, he was transferred to the company's Paris office. He no longer enjoyed the work of selling art. He antagonized customers, often criticizing the choices they made. He took several weeks of vacation around Christmas that year without asking permission. Not surprisingly, he was fired early in 1876.

Except for his broken heart over Eugenie Loyer, he had enjoyed being in England. He decided to go back. He had two low-paying teaching jobs there, but neither one lasted very long.

By this time he was considering a career in the ministry. He was reading the Bible very seriously. While he was still in England, he gave his first sermon. He wrote, "When I was standing in the pulpit, I felt as if, emerging from a dark cave under ground, I had come back to the friendly daylight, and it is a delightful thought that in the future wherever I shall be, I shall preach the Gospel; to do that well, one must have the Gospel in one's heart; may the Lord give it to me."[5]

In 1877 he was back in The Netherlands, where Uncle Cent helped him get a job in a bookstore. Although it fit in with his love of reading, the job lasted for only a few months. He then decided to go to the theological academy in Amsterdam. Many of his relatives lived in the capital city, and they tried to support him.

In the end, Vincent didn't agree with the six-year course of study. He didn't want to spend so much time learning subjects such as Latin, Greek, and mathematics when his main goal was to serve people directly. He dropped out after a little over a year.

He still wanted to help poor people, so he decided to take a direct approach. He received an appointment as a lay preacher in the Borinage, a coal-mining region between Belgium and France. The miners lived and worked in horrible, dangerous conditions. While Vincent wasn't a miner himself, he wanted to live the same way the people did. He gave away most of his possessions, ate little, and slept in shacks.

In an effort to ease the difficulty of his living conditions, Vincent turned to drawing more seriously. He made numerous sketches of the miners and the harsh environment in which they lived. He also copied some of the works of Jean-François Millet. Millet was especially noted for capturing the nobility in peasants. For Van Gogh, this nobility seemed natural. He believed that the poorest people were often the best.

From the point of view of Van Gogh's sponsors, the way that he had chosen to live was unacceptable, and he was fired. It's not clear what he did for the next nine months, as he had little communication with Theo. He was apparently very unhappy. It seemed that he had failed in everything he had tried. But sometime in 1880, he had the most profound epiphany of his life.

In a letter to Theo, he explained, "I am good for something; my life has an aim after all; I know that I might be quite a different man! There is something inside of me; what can it be?"[6]

Jean-François Millet

Jean-François Millet was born in the French province of Normandy in 1814. His parents were farmers. At first it appeared that their son would follow them into the fields. At the age of twenty he left the farm to study painting in the city of Cherbourg. Three years later he received a scholarship to study in Paris.

The Gleaners, painted by Millet in 1857

At first he painted in the style of the time. He used subjects from mythology and made conventional portraits of well-to-do people.

In 1849, he moved to Barbizon, a rural area near Paris, and began painting the peasants there. He wasn't the first painter to depict peasants, but he was the first to show that they could be just as dignified and important as people who were supposedly their betters.

One of his most noted works is *The Gleaners.* Gleaners were people who combed the fields after the harvest, looking for stray grains of wheat. It was a very low status job. Yet Millet's gleaners, even though they are bent over, approach their seemingly degrading task with a concentration that gives their work importance.

Another famous painting is *The Angelus.* It shows a peasant couple in silent prayer at sunset. They stand in apparent respect for a peaceful, unchanging nature. As is the case with Millet's other peasant figures, they are presented with dignity. There is no hint of poverty or need about them. Soon they will go home, eat their dinner, and rest up for the following day's work.

The Angelus had a particularly strong impact on Van Gogh. "That's magnificent, that's poetry,"[7] he wrote to Theo when he saw it for the first time.

Millet continued to live and work in Barbizon for the rest of his life. He died there in 1875.

For Your Information

Painted in 1885, *The Potato Eaters* is considered to be Van Gogh's first masterpiece. It depicts a peasant family eating dinner after a hard day of work. He deliberately chose subjects whom some people would consider ugly, because they were natural, living in harmony with their environment. The painting hangs in the Van Gogh Museum in Amsterdam, The Netherlands.

three

Becoming an Artist

Not long after he wondered what was "inside" him, Van Gogh answered his own question. He walked nearly forty miles to show his drawings to a famous artist named Jules Breton. But when he arrived at Breton's house, he lost his nerve. Without even trying to approach the artist, he turned around and headed back. It was a miserable trip. He wrote:

> I earned some crusts of bread along the road here and there in exchange for some drawings which I had in my valise," he wrote. "But I had to spend the last nights in the open air, once in an abandoned wagon which was white with frost the next morning . . . and once, that was a little better, in a haystack, where I succeeded in making a rather more comfortable berth, but then a drizzling rain did not exactly further my well-being.
>
> Well, it was even in that deep misery that I felt my energy revive and that I said to myself: In spite of everything I shall rise again; I will take up my pencil, which I have forsaken in my great discouragement, and I will go on with my drawing; and from that moment everything seemed transformed; and now I have started. . . . It was the too long and too great poverty which had discouraged me so much that I could not do anything.[1]

"At last he had found his work," adds Van Gogh-Bonger, "and his mental equilibrium was restored; he no longer doubted himself, and however difficult or hard his life became, the inner serenity, the conviction of having found his own calling, never deserted him again."[2]

He thought that he needed formal classes, so in October 1880 he enrolled at the Brussels Art Academy in Belgium. He was too independent to take instruction and quickly dropped out. That same month he received a break. Theo had been working for Goupil in Paris, and his career was going well. He began sending Vincent some money on which to live each month. For nearly the rest of Vincent's life, Theo's generosity would be his sole source of income.

The following spring he moved home for a few months. His father had been transferred to a new parish at Etten, not far from Vincent's birthplace. There, Vincent had another unfortunate love affair. His slightly older cousin Kee Vos-Stricker had recently been widowed. She had an eight-year-old son. At first Kee thought that the attention Vincent was paying to her was on account of her son. She soon learned otherwise.

He said that he was deeply in love with her. She wanted no part of him, but Vincent refused to give up. Once he even put his hand into the flame of a candle when he was visiting her parents. He said he wouldn't take it out until she spoke to him. Her father quickly blew out the candle before Vincent could do lasting damage to himself.

Many scholars believe that this relationship marked another turning point in his life. It apparently convinced him that he could never truly have a loving relationship with a woman.

At the start of 1882, he moved to The Hague. He wanted to work with Anton Mauve, a well-known painter who was married to one of his cousins.

Vincent used most of the money Theo had sent to pay for models and painting supplies. A few months later he began living with a poor woman named Sien Hoornik. She had one small child and was pregnant with another. It was a very scandalous relationship. No one he knew approved of it. Still, Vincent stayed with her for more than a year.

Finally he left Sien Hoornik and spent a few months in the province of Drente, where he lived by himself. Vincent was especially depressed

Many art critics believe that *Skull of a Skeleton with Burning Cigarette*, painted in 1886, is Van Gogh's comment on the conservative art world of his era, which largely ignored him.

and felt guilty about abandoning Sien. He was also concerned that Theo's generous assistance provided the only way in which he could survive.

Then he moved back in with his parents. They tried to support and understand him, and they even provided him with a studio. But he was very difficult to get along with. Then his mother fell and broke her leg. Vincent took over much of her care, which helped bring the family closer together.

Vincent's father died in March 1885. Shortly before his death, he had moved to yet another parish, this one in the village of Nuenen. Without his father's sheltering influence, life in Nuenen became difficult for Vincent. He was a virtual stranger to the villagers and didn't fit in with them. His behavior was often unpredictable and they couldn't understand his devotion to his art.

The first phase of his artistic career was about to reach its climax. He had always admired poor people for their endurance, and his work so far had featured them. Now he was putting the finishing touches on a large painting he called *The Potato Eaters*. He thought it was excellent. In his opinion, "I have tried to make it clear how these people, eating their potatoes under the lamplight, have dug the earth with those very hands

they put in the dish; and so the painting speaks of manual labor, and how they have honestly earned their food. I wanted to give the impression of quite a different way of living than that of us civilized people."[3]

He emphasized that the work was more effective by showing the people in the way that they normally dressed and lived rather than "dressing it up" to make it more appealing commercially.

"I for my part am convinced that I get better results by painting [peasants] in their roughness than by giving them a conventional charm," he told Theo. "I think a peasant girl is beautiful in her dusty and patched blue petticoat. . . . If she puts on a lady's dress she loses her typical charm. . . . To paint peasant life is a serious thing, and I should reproach myself if I did not try to make pictures which raise serious thoughts in those who think seriously about art and about life."[4]

Van Gogh would always be true to this philosophy of painting—raising serious thoughts—whether his subject was peasants or picturesque landscapes. In the meantime, his own generation wouldn't appreciate what he was doing.

In November he moved yet again, this time to Antwerp, Belgium. He lived as cheaply as possible, in the attic of a house. He began experimenting

One of Van Gogh's earliest works, probably from 1883, *Flower Beds in Holland* shows the interest in color and texture that he developed in his later paintings. It is part of the Mellon Collection of the National Gallery of Art in Washington, D.C.

with different painting techniques. He also began to study Japanese art, especially by printmakers such as Hiroshige and Hokusai. The Japanese featured unusual compositions of their subjects and used large blocks of individual colors. Van Gogh's work began to take on the bold coloration of these works.

A few months later he moved to Paris and began living with Theo, now a successful and established art dealer. There he became acquainted with the works of the Impressionists. They were a group of painters who had revolutionized the art world. They used bright, vibrant colors and often painted outdoor landscapes. Almost overnight Van Gogh abandoned his dark colors and his peasant subjects. Now he too was creating very colorful paintings.

In 1888, Van Gogh created a series of paintings to show sunflowers in several stages, ranging from being fully in bloom to withering. This is one of two very similar works entitled *Still Life: Vase with Twelve Flowers.* There are also three named *Still Life: Vase with Fifteen Flowers.* One of these is the painting that set the $40 million record that *Irises* and then *Portrait of Dr. Gachet* broke.

His time in Paris also contained a downside. His health, which had never been good because he rarely ate very well, became even worse. He drank too much coffee and too much alcohol. He became so irritable that even Theo had a hard time getting along with him.

Painted in 1889, *Bedroom in Arles* (third verson) shows Van Gogh's sleeping chamber in a house he rented. He intended to create a restful atmosphere by the colors he chose. Some people believe that its emptiness shows Van Gogh's desire for companionship.

Not long after the two brothers began living together, Theo wrote to their sister Willemina, "My home life is unbearable. Nobody wants to come and see me any more because it always ends in quarrels, and besides, he is untidy, his room always looks so unattractive. I wish he would go and live by himself. . . . It seems as if he were two persons: one marvelously gifted, tender, and refined; the other egotistic and hard-hearted. They present themselves in turns, so that one hears him talk first in one way, then in the other, and always with arguments on both sides. It is a pity he is his own enemy, for he makes life hard, not only for others, but for himself."[5]

Somehow they managed to live together for more than a year after Theo wrote the letter. These disagreements didn't affect Vincent's output. Scholars estimate that he completed nearly 200 paintings during the time that he lived in Paris.

But he wanted to move on. Even with the benefit of his brother's steady company, the pace of life in Paris was too hectic. For Vincent, that could mean only one direction: south.

Impressionism

For many years, France was the center of the art world. French painters, who did all their work in studios, tried to be as "realistic" as possible. Their intent was to show their subjects as they really existed. They tried to eliminate any trace of brushstrokes. They also concentrated on "important" subjects, such as historical events, popular episodes in mythology, and notable people.

Monet's Impression: Sunrise

In the 1860s, a group of artists rebelled against these strict standards. They wanted to create art that was more spontaneous and colorful. This group included Edouard Manet, Alfred Sisley, Claude Monet, Pierre-Auguste Renoir, Camille Pissarro, and Edgar Degas. In 1874 they organized an exhibition to showcase their paintings. A famous art critic didn't approve of what he saw. He especially didn't like one of Monet's works, called *Impression: Sunrise.* He claimed that it didn't seem like a finished painting. It was more like a quick sketch. As a putdown, he called Monet and the others "impressionists."

Out of spite, the group decided to adopt the name. Soon the Impressionists became the most important painters in France. They had several things in common.

First, they painted outdoors. That enabled them to fully appreciate and capture the changing effects of natural light under different conditions. They also used lighter and brighter colors than painters who had preceded them.

They emphasized their brushstrokes rather than trying to conceal them. One popular method was to employ short, choppy strokes that gave the painting a somewhat dreamlike quality. This technique created a certain feeling rather than clearly showing details.

Their subjects came from ordinary life. A family having a picnic, a railroad station, even haystacks or water lilies took on new importance by the way in which they were depicted.

Impressionism soon lost its influence among painters. It was succeeded by movements such as Post-Impressionism and Cubism. However, Impressionist paintings remain very popular among the general public, and their exhibitions continue to draw large crowds of art lovers.

For Your Information

Soon after arriving in Arles in 1888, Van Gogh heard of the death of Anton Mauve. Van Gogh had briefly studied with Mauve and remained fond of him. He dedicated his first painting in Arles, *Peach Tree in Bloom*, to Mauve's memory. The line in the lower left-hand corner says, *"Souvenir de Mauve."*

four

Into the Sunshine

Van Gogh moved south to Arles, France, in February 1888. Located on the Rhone River, the city was less than twenty miles from the Mediterranean Sea.

Noted art historian Ingo Walther emphasizes, "The fascination of the south . . . the fascination which the Mediterranean landscapes held for northern artists, with its mild climate and warm sun bathing the landscape in radiant light. The consequences of the 'artists' pilgrimage' can be seen in the paintings themselves: the palettes become more colorful, the colors brighter, the themes recalled the antique age."[1]

At first Van Gogh was shocked. Instead of sun, he was greeted by snow. It was the coldest winter in Arles in nearly thirty years.

In less than a month the snow was gone. Van Gogh was dazzled by the bright sunlight and the beautiful country scenes. He began painting rapidly and soon developed his own unique style. It involved heavy bright colors, many of which he mixed on the spot.

One of his first paintings after the sun came out was *Peach Tree in Bloom*. Fruit trees were a favorite subject of Japanese artists. Seeing these trees, Van Gogh felt almost as if he was able to experience a Japanese landscape firsthand. "This country seems to be as beautiful as Japan as far as the limpidity of the atmosphere and the gay color effects are concerned,"[2] he wrote. The blooms on the tree represented his own optimism. He thought that finally he was about to enjoy his life. Painting enabled him to do that.

In May, he rented a small house he called the Yellow House because of its color. He dreamed of making it an artists' colony so that artists could band together. They would exchange ideas and encourage one another. A few months later Paul Gauguin, another relatively unknown painter, said that he would join him. Theo was helping Gauguin sell his paintings, but so far he hadn't been very successful. In preparation for Gaugin's arrival, Van Gogh created one of his most famous series, several paintings of sunflowers. They would decorate the walls for Gauguin and provide inspiration for both men.

At first all went well. Van Gogh was delighted to have someone to talk to who understood his passion for art. The two men worked together, painting side by side, and spent their evenings having long discussions.

Then Gauguin started acting as if he were the better painter. The two men got into bitter arguments.

Van Gogh painted two pictures of chairs that show how different the two men were. Gauguin's chair *(Gauguin's Armchair)* is elegant and elaborate. It contains an ornate candlestick and two contemporary novels. The lighting comes from a candle on the wall.

By contrast, in *Vincent's Chair with His Pipe,* Van Gogh's chair is made of wicker, a very ordinary material. It holds just his pipe and tobacco. Behind it, an onion inside a wooden box is sprouting. The room is flooded with natural sunlight. The contrast between the paintings suggests that Van Gogh felt he was closer to the earth and to "real life."

In December, Theo wrote with momentous news. He was getting married to a woman named Johanna Bonger.

Vincent wasn't entirely happy with the news. He may have been jealous that someone else would now come first with his brother. On top of that, his disagreements with Gauguin were getting worse and worse. On December 23, they had an especially violent quarrel.

No one is sure about the sequence of events that followed. Gauguin later said that Van Gogh threatened him with a sharp razor. Van Gogh never said anything about it. But one thing is clear: In a fit of extremely violent temper, Vincent van Gogh sliced off part of his left ear. He wrapped

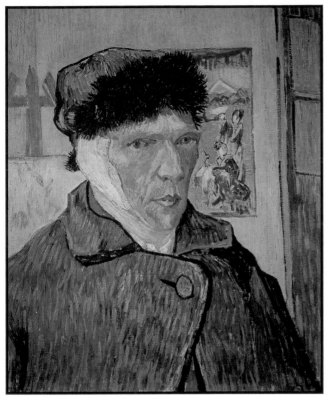

Even though Van Gogh cut off part of his left ear, *Self-Portrait with Bandaged Ear* shows a bandage over his right ear. This suggests that Van Gogh was looking in a mirror and painted what he saw there. According to one version of the story, Van Gogh thought he heard a voice telling him to kill Gauguin, and he cut off the ear so that he wouldn't have to listen anymore.

it in a handkerchief, ran outside, and gave it to a woman he knew. She was horrified and called the police.

They found Vincent lying unconscious on his bed. He was taken to the hospital, where he had to stay for nearly two weeks. It was the beginning of recurrent episodes of depression and melancholy that would completely incapacitate him for days or even weeks at a time. While at the hospital, he was treated by Dr. Felix Rey, who believed that Van Gogh suffered from epilepsy. This is a disease characterized by loss of consciousness and convulsive fits. Van Gogh soon used Dr. Rey as the subject of one of his paintings, portraying him with a red beard and green hair. Rey's parents were so horrified that they used it to patch their chicken coop. Somehow it managed to survive and now hangs in a museum in Russia.

Since then, many people have suggested other causes of Van Gogh's mental instability. Some modern medical researchers believe that Van Gogh may have suffered from bipolar disorder. This mental illness is characterized by periods of depression followed by periods of exhilaration, called mania. Sufferers in the manic stage may experience paranoia, and they often feel as if they do not need to eat or sleep. Sometimes Van Gogh would hallucinate, believing that imaginary people were speaking to him. He also believed that people were trying to kill him.

His intense work habits provide another clue. From the time of his missionary work in the Borinage, he had always thrown himself completely into what he did. His work was far more important to him than his health. He was even more prolific in Arles than he had been in Paris. In just over a year after leaving Paris, he completed nearly 200 paintings and dozens of drawings.

As he explained to Theo, "Today again, from seven o'clock in the morning till six in the evening, I worked without stirring to eat a bite a step or two away. That is why the work is getting on fast. . . . I have lived for four days on twenty-three cups of coffee, with bread for which I still owe. And I have left today for the week, and after four days of strict fasting at that, just six francs. I ate at noon, but this evening I shall sup on a crust of bread."[3] His lack of food contributed to his run-down condition.

Soon after Theo and Jo were married in April 1889, Vincent was again severely depressed. This time he chose to go to a private clinic, at nearby Saint-Rémy. He wrote to his sister Willemina, "I am going to an asylum in Saint-Rémy, not far from here, for four months. I have had in all four great crises, during which I didn't in the least know what I said, what I wanted and what I did. . . . I am unable to describe exactly what is the matter with me; now and then there are horrible fits of anxiety, apparently without cause, or otherwise a feeling of emptiness and fatigue in the head. . . . Every day I take the remedy which the incomparable [Charles] Dickens [a famous English author] prescribes against suicide. It consists of a glass of wine, a piece of bread with cheese and a pipe of tobacco."[4]

He did ask for one concession on being admitted: that he would still be allowed to paint. He wasn't insane, he argued; no madman could have painted the way he did or written such thoughtful, intelligent letters. Because there were many empty rooms, he received permission to make one of them into a studio.

Life in the clinic wasn't always easy. "I feel like a fool to go and ask permission from doctors to make pictures," he complained to Theo. "The

Starry Night is one of Van Gogh's "signature" paintings, one that nearly everyone who is familiar with the artist recognizes at once. He stayed up for three nights in a row to paint it. The contrast between the turbulent sky and the calm earth represents Van Gogh's turmoil and his desire for inner peace. Some people believe that the tall cypress tree in the left of the painting is a symbol of a pathway to heaven.

work on my pictures seems essential to my recovery, for these days without anything to do, and without being able to go to the room they had allotted to me to do my painting in, are almost intolerable. Work strengthens the will, and consequently leaves less hold for my mental weakness; it distracts me infinitely better than anything else. If I could once really throw myself into it with all my heart it might be the best remedy."[5]

From his window he could see many scenes, though he always painted them without the bars on the windows. One of his most famous paintings, *Starry Night,* was painted from behind those bars. It contrasts the calmness of the earth with a turbulent night sky. The stars are portrayed in a series of whirls. The effect is almost dizzying. There is also a nod to his long-vanished boyhood. The church steeple, which is the most dominant feature of the landscape, wasn't part of the actual view. The steeple was from one of the churches he had known when he was growing up in The Netherlands.

At other times he was allowed to go outside. He painted *Irises* in the garden of the asylum. This was the painting that would later set an auction record.

Being at Saint-Rémy was a mixed blessing. Van Gogh was somewhat at peace and able to paint, yet he continued to push himself far too hard. On at least one occasion, he ate some of his paint. It contained lead, which is poisonous and can cause brain damage.

He believed that he was making progress mentally. He wanted to leave Saint-Rémy, yet he didn't trust himself to live alone. The painter Camille Pissarro had an idea. A physician named Paul-Ferdinand Gachet lived in the small town of Auvers-sur-Oise. The doctor was interested in painting and had treated several painters. He would be sympathetic to Van Gogh's condition and would work with him.

In May 1890, Van Gogh left Saint-Rémy. The hospital director marked him as "cured." He may have been—for the moment.

Paul Gauguin

Paul Gauguin was born in 1848 in Paris. When he was just one, his family moved to Peru, his mother's home. His father, who had gotten in trouble with the French government, died during the voyage across the Atlantic Ocean.

Paul, his mother, and his sister lived with wealthy relatives in Peru until the boy was seven. Then they moved back to France. Paul went to school there. Ten years later, he joined the French merchant marine. In 1868, he became a member of the French Navy.

Shortly after leaving the navy in 1871, he began working for a stockbroker. It is likely that he also began his first experiments with drawing and painting. With the money that he made as a stockbroker, he could afford to buy paintings by other artists. In 1873 he married a Danish woman named Mette Sophie Gadd. Eventually they would have five children.

Gauguin became more and more involved with his artwork. In 1884 he moved to Copenhagen, Denmark, with his family. Five months later he abandoned them so that, he reasoned, he could concentrate on becoming an artist. He moved to Paris, where he met Vincent van Gogh.

Paul Gauguin's *Self Portrait with Halo* dates to 1889. He once wrote, "Life is hardly more than a fraction of a second. Such a little time to prepare oneself for eternity!"

In 1891 he decided to abandon European civilization altogether. He wanted a simpler lifestyle and the chance to find peace of mind. He moved to Tahiti, but returned to France two years later because of a serious illness. He returned to the South Pacific in 1895 for good.

Many of his most famous works were painted over the next eight years. They show various scenes in the South Pacific islands. He became especially known for his use of warm, rich colors and symbols that were personally important.

Yet Gauguin never seemed to be happy. He tried to commit suicide in 1897. Four years later, he was seriously ill again. He had also gotten into trouble with the French authorities who controlled Tahiti. He moved to the Marquesas Islands, where he died in May of 1903.

Starry Night over the Rhone shows Van Gogh's interest in the challenges of painting at night. He was especially fascinated by the reflections of gas lights, which were relatively new. The constellation that dominates the upper center of the painting is the Big Dipper (Ursa Major), but from this vantage point it would actually be behind the observer.

five

The Final Hours—and Future Fame

Van Gogh boarded a train and journeyed back to Paris. He saw his nephew, Vincent Willem van Gogh, for the first time. The little boy had been named for him.

Several days later, he set off for Auvers and Dr. Gachet. He immediately liked the little town. "Auvers is very beautiful," he wrote Theo. "One is far enough from Paris for it to be real country. . . . There is a lot to draw here, and there is much color . . . it is profoundly beautiful; it is the real country, characteristic and picturesque."[1]

Soon he added, "Doctor Gachet said that I must work boldly only and not think at all of what went wrong with me."[2]

There can be little doubt that he took the doctor's words to heart. Inspired by the scenery, he went to work. In just over two months, he created nearly seventy new paintings.

He felt like he was at the top of his game and had become a master of his art. He continued to work at great speed. While the colors were still vivid, there was now a darker palette and the brushstrokes became more violent.

Dr. Gachet often had Van Gogh over for dinner. It seemed like he was finally able to relax. Yet within two months, Van Gogh again showed signs of depression. It didn't help that Theo had his problems as well. He and his baby were often ill. Johanna was rapidly becoming exhausted with caring for them.

Perhaps Van Gogh felt finally abandoned. By this time his relationship with Dr. Gachet had cooled. He once threatened the doctor with a pistol because he hadn't framed some of his paintings.

Yet as always he managed to paint. Many scholars believe that his last great masterpiece—perhaps his last painting ever—*Wheatfield with Crows*, was painted sometime in mid- to late July. Perhaps startled by a boom of thunder, a flock of crows rises above a wheat field and begins to fly away. Van Gogh recognized the power and the meaning of the painting. He referred to "vast stretches of wheat under troubled skies,

The Café Terrace on the Place du Forum was the first painting in which Van Gogh used a starry background. Painted in 1888, it is one of his most colorful works. Today the Café Terrace is known as the Café Van Gogh.

Wheatfield with Crows is among Van Gogh's final paintings and offers clues to his state of mind. The dark sky is ominous, the many crows are symbols of death, and the road in the center ends very abruptly. Nor are there any humans present.

and I did not need to go out of my way to try to express sadness and the extremity of loneliness."[3]

As art historians Josephine Cutts and James Smith note, "The painting undoubtedly reflects elements of Van Gogh's extreme melancholy. A major source of his depression was the fact that he remained a financial burden to Theo, who now had a son to support. The vigorous, frustrated brushstrokes bear witness to his troubled mind."[4]

On July 23, Vincent wrote his final letter to his brother: "I should rather like to write to you about a lot of things, but to begin with, the desire to do it has left me completely, and again I feel it is useless. I still love art and life very much, but as for ever having a wife of my own, I have no great faith in that. I am—at least I feel—too old to go back on my steps or to desire anything different. That desire has left me, though the mental suffering from it remains."[5]

Van Gogh asked to be admitted to an asylum at Saint-Rémy in May 1889. It's likely that he painted *Trees in the Asylum Garden* soon after his arrival. In all, he completed more than 150 paintings and drawings during the year he spent there.

Four days later, he walked into the wheat fields and shot himself in the chest with a pistol. The bullet didn't kill him. He managed to stagger back to the inn where he was staying and go up to his room.

The innkeeper went to check on him, and Van Gogh confessed what he had done. The bullet was near his heart and couldn't be removed. Van Gogh was dying. The innkeeper desperately summoned Dr. Gachet, who in turn wrote to Theo. Theo hurried to his brother's side. He was still there when Vincent died on July 29, 1890. The artist was only thirty-seven years old.

As Theo wrote to his wife, "One of his last words was, 'I wish I could pass away like this,' and his wish was fulfilled. A few moments and all was over. He had found the rest he could not find on earth."[6]

Vincent van Gogh often saw his life as a complete failure. He never married or had any children. He was fired from what seemed to be a good career as an art dealer. He tried and failed to become a minister. He worked briefly as a teacher and a bookseller. At the time of his death, his art was almost unnoticed.

In fact, Van Gogh had become a successful artist. He had broken new ground in several areas: landscapes, still lifes, interiors, and portraits. In particular, the number and quality of his self-portraits are especially notable.

The dozens of masterpieces he created in a short period of time—from *The Potato Eaters* in 1885 to *The Portrait of Dr. Gachet* and *Wheatfield with Crows* just over five years later—is truly remarkable. His unique style is instantly recognizable. His name on an exhibition of paintings assures huge crowds and long lines. Perhaps one reason for his appeal is the obvious excitement he felt while he painted. Clearly he poured everything he had—physically, mentally, and spiritually—into his art. He wrote, "It is the excitement, the honesty of a man of nature, led by

Van Gogh began *Village Street in Auvers* in May 1890, a few weeks before his death. Uncharacteristically, he never completed it. The painting lacks the swirling brushstrokes that were typical of much of his final works.

nature's hand. And sometimes this excitement is so strong that one works without noticing it— the strokes of the brush come in quick succession and lead on from one to the next like words in a conversation or letter."[7]

Ravaged by physical ailments, exhaustion, and his own emotional turmoil, Theo followed his brother in death six months later. Johanna decided to preserve the works and reputation of her brother-in-law. She worked tirelessly to arrange exhibitions, which would open within a few years. Van Gogh, who sold only one painting in his life, would have been astonished to see how many of his works were selling— and the prices that people were willing to pay for them.

Van Gogh painted *Self-Portrait without Beard* for his mother in September 1889. Besides showing the artist as clean-shaven, it also shows him with an undamaged left ear. At an auction in 1998, it sold for $71.5 million.

The exhibitions and the climbing prices for his paintings continue. As the stories of *Irises, Sunflowers,* and *Portrait of Dr. Gachet* illustrate, his paintings are among the highest-valued in the world today.

"The more I think of it, the more I think Vincent was a giant," Dr. Gachet told Theo a few days after his brother's funeral. "Not a day passes that I do not look at his pictures. I always find there a new idea, something different each day. . . . I think again of the painter and I find him a colossus."[8]

It is a judgment with which nearly everyone who sees the paintings of Vincent van Gogh today would agree.

Self-Portraits

It's likely that no other artist has focused so much on painting himself as Vincent van Gogh. Noted Dutch painter Rembrandt actually depicted himself more often—in sixty paintings and twenty engravings—than Van Gogh, who has about forty surviving self-portraits. However, Rembrandt's career lasted much longer, about four decades. All of Van Gogh's self-portraits were generated over a four-year span. One reason he did so many was to experiment with different techniques. He would then use these techniques in his other work.

There is another difference between the two men. Rembrandt lived in an era long before photography. Van Gogh, on the other hand, lived when photography had become well established. Yet there are only three posed photographs of him, and some authorities believe that even those are of someone else, most likely his brother. As he explained to his sister Willemina, "These photographic portraits wither much sooner than we ourselves do, whereas the painted portrait is a thing which is felt, done with love or respect for the human being that is portrayed."[9]

There may have been another reason for his distaste for photography. When he painted himself, he could control the emotions he wanted to express. Some of the portraits show the way that he wanted to see himself rather than the way he actually was. For example, when he first moved to Paris, he wanted to appear respectable. He wore good clothing and appears very confident in several of these portraits.

His later self-portraits clearly reveal his impending breakdown. What is probably the final one—painted in 1889—was a seventieth birthday present to his mother. He wanted to reassure her that everything was fine with him. As a result, he portrayed himself as clean-shaven—much as he had appeared as a young man. But he didn't disguise the uneasiness and the haunted look in his eyes.

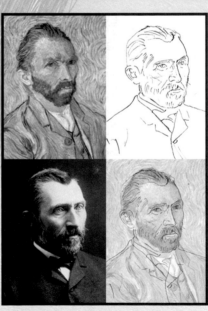

Photograph and self-portrait of Van Gogh compared to one another

1853	Vincent van Gogh is born in Groot-Zundert, the Netherlands, on March 30
1857	His brother Theo is born on May 1
1864	Vincent is sent to boarding school in Zevenbergen
1866	He enters boarding school in Tilburg
1869	He begins working for Goupil & Company in The Hague
1873	Transfers to Goupil's London office
1874	Falls in love with Eugenie Loyer
1875	Transfers to Goupil's Paris office
1876	Is fired from Goupil; moves to England
1877	Begins theological studies in Amsterdam
1878	Leaves school in Amsterdam; begins working as lay preacher in Borinage
1880	Decides to become an artist; Theo begins supporting him financially
1881	Moves to Etten; falls in love with cousin Kee Vos-Stricker
1882	Moves to The Hague; begins living with Sien Hoornik
1883	Leaves Sien Hoornik; lives with his parents in Nuenen
1885	
March	Father dies of a stroke
May	Paints *The Potato Eaters*
Nov.	Moves to Antwerp, Belgium
1886	Moves to Paris and lives with Theo
1888	
Feb.	Moves to Arles in the south of France
May	Rents the Yellow House
Aug.	Paints *Sunflower* series
Oct.	Paul Gauguin moves in with him
Dec.	Cuts off part of his ear; enters Arles hospital, where he is treated by Dr. Felix Rey
1889	Enters mental asylum at St.-Rémy
1890	
Feb.	Sells *The Red Vineyard,* his only formal sale during his lifetime
May	Leaves St.-Rémy; moves to village of Auvers-sur-Oise, where he is treated by Dr. Paul Gachet
June	Paints *Portrait of Dr. Gachet*
July 29	Dies of self-inflicted gunshot wound

1789	The U.S. Constitution is adopted. French Revolution begins.
1803	Louisiana Purchase doubles the size of the new United States.
1818	American ship *Savannah* becomes the first steamship to cross the Atlantic Ocean.
1837	Victoria becomes Queen of England and rules until 1901, the longest reign in English history.
1848	Painter Paul Gauguin is born.
1861	U.S. Civil War begins.
1862	Mexican troops defeat invading French army on May 5, which begins the tradition of Cinco de Mayo.
1865	President Abraham Lincoln is assassinated; the Civil War ends.
1867	Russia sells Alaska to the United States.
1869	Transcontinental railroad in the United States is completed.
1874	Impressionist painters hold their first public exhibition, in Paris.
1879	German physicist Albert Einstein is born.
1883	Brooklyn Bridge opens to traffic in New York City.
1886	Novelist Robert Louis Stevenson writes *Dr. Jekyll and Mr. Hyde.*
1887	Arthur Conan Doyle publishes *A Study in Scarlet,* the first Sherlock Holmes mystery.
1890	Idaho and Wyoming are admitted to the United States.
1895	The first game of professional football is played in Latrobe, Pennsylvania.
1896	First modern Olympic Games are held in Athens, Greece.
1904	Work begins on the Panama Canal; it opens ten years later.
1912	Ocean liner *S.S. Titanic* sinks on its maiden voyage across the Atlantic.
1914	World War I begins.
1918	World War I ends.
1929	The Great Depression begins.
1939	World War II begins.
1945	World War II ends; the United Nations is formed.
1973	The Rijksmuseum Vincent van Gogh opens in Amsterdam.
1990	Van Gogh's *Portrait of Dr. Gachet* sells at an auction for $82.5 million.
2007	A museum in Croatia finds an oil painting signed by "Vincent." They believe it is a previously unknown work by Vincent van Gogh, painted around 1882.

Chapter 1. A Record-Breaking Painting

1. Cynthia Saltzman, *Portrait of Dr. Gachet: The Story of a Van Gogh Masterpiece* (New York: Viking Books, 1998), p. 310.

2. Ibid., p. 31.

3. Ibid.

4. Ibid., p. 35.

5. Ibid., p. xviii.

6. Ibid., p. 42

7. Ingo F. Walther, *Vincent Van Gogh,* translated by Valerie Coyle and Axel Molinski (Cologne, Germany: Benedikt Taschen, 1987), p. 82.

8. Saltzman, p. 36.

Chapter 2. Early Struggles

1. Johanna van Gogh-Bonger, "Memoir of Vincent van Gogh." http://webexhibits.org/vangogh/memoir/sisterinlaw/3.html

2. Ibid.

3. Vincent van Gogh, *Dear Theo: The Autobiography of Vincent van Gogh,* edited by Irving Stone (New York: Plume, 1995), p. 11.

4. Ibid., p. 12.

5. Ibid., p. 19.

6. Ibid., p. 48.

7. Cynthia Saltzman, *Portrait of Dr. Gachet: The Story of a Van Gogh Masterpiece* (New York: Viking Books, 1998), p. 8.

Chapter 3. Becoming an Artist

1. Vincent van Gogh, *Dear Theo: The Autobiography of Vincent van Gogh,* edited by Irving Stone (New York: Plume, 1995), pp. 50–51.

2. Johanna van Gogh-Bonger, "Memoir of Vincent van Gogh." http://webexhibits.org/vangogh/memoir/sisterinlaw/5.html

3. Van Gogh, p. 290.

4. Ibid., pp. 290–291.

5. Bernard Denvir, *Vincent: A Complete Portrait* (Philadelphia: Running Press, 1994), p. 106.

Chapter 4. Into the Sunshine

1. Ingo F. Walther, *Vincent Van Gogh,* translated by Valerie Coyle and Axel Molinski (Cologne, Germany: Benedikt Taschen, 1987), p. 31.

2. Ronald Pickvance, *Van Gogh in Arles* (New York: Harry N. Abrams, 1984), p. 21.

3. Vincent van Gogh, *Dear Theo: The Autobiography of Vincent van Gogh,* edited by Irving Stone (New York: Plume, 1995), pp. 391–393.

4. Pickvance, p. 30.

5. Van Gogh, p. 440.

Chapter 5. The Final Hours—and Future Fame

1. Vincent van Gogh, *Dear Theo: The Autobiography of Vincent van Gogh,* edited by Irving Stone (New York: Plume, 1995), pp. 469–470.

CHAPTER NOTES

2. Ibid., p. 470.

3. Josephine Cutts and James Smith, *Essential van Gogh* (Bath, England: Parragon Publishing, 2003), p. 254.

4. Ibid.

5. Van Gogh, p. 479.

6. Johanna van Gogh-Bonger, "Memoir of Vincent van Gogh." http://webexhibits.org/vangogh/memoir/sisterinlaw/10.html

7. Ingo F. Walther, *Vincent Van Gogh,* translated by Valerie Coyle and Axel Molinski (Cologne, Germany: Benedikt Taschen, 1987), p. 70.

8. Van Gogh-Bonger.

9. Bernard Denvir, *Vincent: A Complete Portrait* (Philadelphia: Running Press, 1994), p. 8.

FURTHER READING

For Young Adults

Bernard, Bruce. *Van Gogh.* New York: Dorling Kindersley, 1992.

Crispino, Enrica. *Masters of Art: Van Gogh.* New York: Peter Bedrick Books, 1996.

Green, Jen. *Vincent van Gogh.* New York: Franklin Watts, 2002.

Greenberg, Jan, and Sandra Jordan. *Vincent van Gogh: Portrait of an Artist.* New York: Delacorte Press, 2001.

Hughes, Andrew. *Famous Artists: Van Gogh.* New York: Barron's Educational Series, 1994.

Lucas, Eileen. *Vincent van Gogh.* New York: Franklin Watts, 1991.

Rubin, Susan Goldman. *The Yellow House: Vincent van Gogh and Paul Gauguin Side by Side.* New York: Henry N. Abrams, 2001.

Works Consulted

Anderson, Janet. *The Life and Works of Vincent van Gogh.* New York: Shooting Star Press, 1994.

Cutts, Josephine, and James Smith. *Essential van Gogh.* Bath, England: Parragon Publishing, 2003.

Denvir, Bernard. *Vincent: A Complete Portrait.* Philadelphia: Running Press, 1994.

Dorn, Roland, et al. *Van Gogh Face to Face: The Portraits.* New York: Thames and Hudson, 2000.

Kleiner, Carolyn. "Van Gogh's Vanishing Act." *U.S. News and World Report,* July 24, 2000. http://www.usnews.com/usnews/doubleissue/mysteries/portrait.htm

Mühlberger, Richard. *What Makes a Van Gogh a Van Gogh?* New York: Viking, 1993.

Pickvance, Ronald. *Van Gogh in Arles.* New York: Harry N. Abrams, 1984.

Saltzman, Cynthia. *Portrait of Dr. Gachet: The Story of a Van Gogh Masterpiece.* New York: Viking Books, 1998.

Schapiro, Meyer. *Van Gogh.* New York: Henry N. Abrams, 1994.

Van Gogh, Vincent. *Dear Theo: The Autobiography of Vincent van Gogh.* Edited by Irving Stone. New York: Plume, 1995.

Walther, Ingo F. *Vincent Van Gogh.* Translated by Valerie Coyle and Axel Molinski. Cologne, Germany: Benedikt Taschen, 1987.

On the Internet

Van Gogh Museum
http://www3.vangoghmuseum.nl/vgm/index.jsp

The Van Gogh Gallery
http://www.vangoghgallery.com/

Van Gogh's Letters – Unabridged
http://webexhibits.org/vangogh/

The Vincent van Gogh Gallery
http://www.vggallery.com/

Vincent van Gogh—THE Master!
http://www.thehollandring.com/vangogh.htm

WebMuseum: Gogh, Vincent van
http://www.ibiblio.org/wm/paint/auth/gogh/

Jean-François Millet, French Painter
http://www.discoverfrance.net/France/Art/Millet/Millet.shtml

Van Gogh-Bonger, Johanna. "Memoir of Vincent van Gogh."
http://webexhibits.org/vangogh/memoir/sisterinlaw/1.html

art critic—A person who knows a great deal about art and makes judgments about the value of particular works based on his or her knowledge.

client (CLY-unt)—A person who uses the professional services of another person.

colossus (kuh-LAH-suss)—A person or thing of immense size or power.

epiphany (ee-PIH-fuh-nee)—An illuminating discovery or realization.

equilibrium (ee-kwah-LIH-bree-um)—State of balance.

lay preacher—A person who serves as a preacher even though he or she has little or no formal religious training.

limpidity (lim-PIH-duh-tee)—Transparency, peacefulness.

palette (PAA-let)—A thin board that an artist uses to mix paints; also the combination of colors an artist chooses to use for a piece of work.

parsonage (PAR-suh-nij)—The home that a church provides for its minister or pastor.

poverty (PAH-ver-tee)—Having very little money and material possessions.

still life—A painting consisting of a particular arrangement of inanimate objects.

stockbroker (STAHK-broh-ker)—A person who buys and sells stocks (shares in a company) for other people and charges a commission for his or her services.

sup—To eat an evening meal.

valise (vah-LEEZ)—A suitcase.